𝔻𝕂 READERS

Level 2

Dinosaur Dinners
Fire Fighter!
Bugs! Bugs! Bugs!
Slinky, Scaly Snakes!
Animal Hospital
The Little Ballerina
Munching, Crunching, Sniffing,
  and Snooping
The Secret Life of Trees
Winking, Blinking, Wiggling,
  and Waggling
Astronaut: Living in Space
Twisters!

Holiday! Celebration Days
  around the World
The Story of Pocahontas
Horse Show
Survivors: The Night the Titanic Sank
Eruption! The Story of Volcanoes
The Story of Columbus
Journey of a Humpback Whale
Amazing Buildings
LEGO: Castle Under Attack
LEGO: Rocket Rescue
¡Insectos! en español
Ice Skating Stars

Level 3

Spacebusters: The Race to the Moon
Beastly Tales
Shark Attack!
Titanic
Invaders from Outer Space
Movie Magic
Plants Bite Back!
Time Traveler
Bermuda Triangle
Tiger Tales
Aladdin
Heidi
Zeppelin: The Age of the Airship
Spies
Terror on the Amazon
Disasters at Sea

The Story of Anne Frank
Abraham Lincoln: Lawyer, Leader,
  Legend
George Washington: Soldier, Hero,
  President
Extreme Sports
Spiders' Secrets
The Big Dinosaur Dig
Space Heroes: Amazing Astronauts
LEGO: Mission to the Arctic
NFL: Super Bowl Heroes
NFL: Peyton Manning
MLB: Home Run Heroes: Big Mac,
  Sammy, and Junior
MLB: Roberto Clemente
MLB: Roberto Clemente en español
MLB: World Series Heroes

Level 4

Days of the Knights
Volcanoes and Other Natural Disasters
Pirates: Raiders of the High Seas
Horse Heroes
Trojan Horse
Micro Monsters
Going for Gold!
Extreme Machines
Flying Ace: The Story of Amelia Earhart
Robin Hood
Black Beauty
Free at Last! The Story of
  Martin Luther King, Jr.
Joan of Arc
Spooky Spinechillers
Welcome to The Globe! The
  Story of Shakespeare's Theater
Antarctic Adventure
Space Station
Atlantis: The Lost City?
Dinosaur Detectives
Danger on the Mountain: Scaling
  the World's Highest Peaks
Crime Busters

The Story of Muhammad Ali
First Flight: The Story of the Wright
  Brothers
LEGO: Race for Survival
NFL: NFL's Greatest Upsets
NFL: Rumbling Running Backs
WCW: Going for Goldberg
WCW: Feel the Sting
MLB: Strikeout Kings
MLB: Super Shortstops: Jeter,
  Nomar, and A-Rod
MLB: The Story of the New York
  Yankees
JLA: Batman's Guide to the Universe
JLA: Superman's Guide to the Universe
The Story of the X-Men: How it
  all Began
Creating the X-Men: How Comic
  Books Come to Life
Spider-Man's Amazing Powers
The Story of Spider-Man
The Incredible Hulk's Book of Strength
The Story of the Incredible Hulk
Transformers Armada: The Awakening
Transformers Armada: The Quest

A Note to Parents

DK READERS is a compelling program for beginning readers, designed in conjunction with leading literacy experts, including Dr. Linda Gambrell, Director of the School of Education at Clemson University. Dr. Gambrell has served on the Board of Directors of the International Reading Association and as President of the National Reading Conference.

Beautiful illustrations and superb full-color photographs combine with engaging, easy-to-read stories to offer a fresh approach to each subject in the series. Each DK READER is guaranteed to capture a child's interest while developing his or her reading skills, general knowledge, and love of reading.

The five levels of DK READERS are aimed at different reading abilities, enabling you to choose the books that are exactly right for your child:

Pre-level 1: Learning to read
Level 1: Beginning to read
Level 2: Beginning to read alone
Level 3: Reading alone
Level 4: Proficient readers

The "normal" age at which a child begins to read can be anywhere from three to eight years old, so these levels are intended only as a general guideline.

No matter which level you select, you can be sure that you are helping your child learn to read, then read to learn!

LONDON, NEW YORK, MUNICH,
MELBOURNE, AND DELHI

Project Editor Carey Combe
Art Editor Mandy Earey

Senior Editor Linda Esposito
Senior Art Editor
Diane Thistlethwaite
US Editor Regina Kahney
Production Melanie Downing
Picture Researcher Jamie Robertson
Picture Library Rachel Hilford,
Lee Thompson
Illustrator Chris Forsey

Reading Consultant
Linda Gambrell

First American Edition, 2000
04 05 10 9 8
Published in the United States by DK Publishing, Inc.
375 Hudson Street, New York, New York 10014

Published in Great Britain by Dorling Kindersley Limited

Library of Congress Cataloging-in-Publication Data

Platt, Richard.
Spies: / by Richard Platt. – 1st American ed.
p.cm. – (Dorling Kindersley readers)
Summary: Examines the history, motives, and actions of various spies,
both criminal and governmental.
ISBN 0-7894-5712-1 (hc) – ISBN 0-7894-5713-X (pb)
1. Espionage–Juvenile literature. 2. Spies–Juvenile literature.
[1. Espionage. 2. Spies.]
I. Title. II Series.

JF1525.16 P58 2000
327.12–dc21
                                        99-087062
Color reproduction by Colourscan, Singapore
Printed and bound in Belgium by Proost

The publisher would like to thank the following for their kind permission to
reproduce the photographs.
a=above, b=below, c=center, l=left, r=right, t=top.
AKG London: 8tl; Camera Press: 25tr, 25br, 25l; Corbis UK Ltd: Bettmann
16bl; Robert Maas 39t; Dk Picture Library: 18l, 29c, 31br, 34/35; Mary Evans
Picture Library: 9c; Galaxy Picture Library: Robin Scagell 41tr; Ronald Grant
Archive: EON Production 26tl, 26br; Robert Harding Picture Library: Dusty
Willison / International Stock 37t; Hulton Getty: 24tl, 27tr; Military Picture
Library: Robin Adshead 31tl; PA News Photo Library: 17tr; Pictor
International: 38b, 43br; Rex Features: 30b, 31tl, 46/47; The Sun 47tr; Tripett
45t; Science Photo Library: NRSC Ltd 42t; Frank Spooner Pictures: 21c, 23br;
Topham Picturepoint: 10br, 19tr, 22c, 35tr, 40b, 44b.
Jacket: Camera Press: John Philby Front cr; Corbis UK Ltd: Bettmann Front cl;
Pictor International: Back tl, Back tr; Rex Features: Front br.
All other images © Dorling Kindersley Limited.
For further information see: www.dkimages.com

Discover more at
www.dk.com

Contents

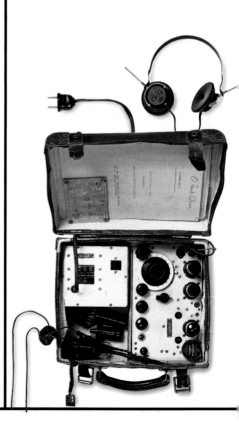

DK READERS

SPIES

Written by Richard Platt

DK Publishing, Inc.

What do spies do?

In a dark office, in an enemy country, a spy breaks open a safe. He removes the plans for a new, top-secret missile. His hands shake. He is breaking the law – risking torture and prison if the guards catch him! With a tiny camera he copies the plans. Quickly he returns the papers and silently escapes. No one has seen him – the mission is a success!

This spy is helping to protect his country. The stolen pictures will help his country's scientists design defenses against the enemy weapon. But spies do many other jobs. Some work in their home country to keep it safe from terrorists. A few are secret killers. Many more guard their own country's secrets and protect them from enemy spies.

Ancient spies at work

There have been spies since ancient times. A Bible story tells how spies sneaked into Jericho, a town in Jordan, to learn about its defenses.

Spies spy for lots of different reasons. High pay attracts many of them. Others spy against their own country because they disagree with its rulers. Some spy because they have been blackmailed. They don't want to spy, but an enemy spy has threatened to reveal a shameful secret unless they spy for him. Others start to spy just because they love the excitement involved. Living a secret, sometimes dangerous, life thrills them.

Many spy because they believe the information they collect on evil rulers helps make the world a safer place.

But spies don't always spy for a country. Businesses use spies, too. Businesses want to know the secrets of their rivals. Industrial spying is very important. By stealing technical and electronic secrets from rivals, companies can make the same product but at a lower price.

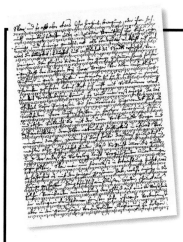

Spies have always had to work in secret. To help them do this, they write important messages in code. Codes turn messages into a jumble of letters that look like nonsense – hiding the original meaning. Only the sender and receiver know how to read the secret code.

Roman emperor Julius Caesar used a simple code to send messages to Rome more than 2,000 years ago. He moved each letter forward three places in the alphabet. So A became D, B became E, and so on. Written in this code, Caesar's name becomes FDHVDU.

Codes like this are simple to crack because each letter in the code stands for the same letter of the real message.

A code is like a lock – you have to find the right key. But unlike Caesar's code, modern codes are very tough to unlock.

Caesar's success in battle was partly a result of the information his spies collected about the enemy.

When the punishment for spying is death, spies will sometimes kill to avoid capture. Other spies are sent on deadly murder missions by their bosses.

Spies in 16th-century Venice killed with glass daggers. Once they stabbed their victim the blade snapped off in the body, ensuring a certain death. The only clue that remained was a tiny cut.

The deadliest killers of all were the 12th-century Japanese spies known as Ninja "invisible men." Dressed in black, they crept silently into houses to poison or stab their poor, unsuspecting victims.

Modern murder
Spies still kill. In 1978 Bulgarian Georgi Markov was killed by a spy using a special gun hidden in an umbrella.

It was said that no guard could stop a Ninja attack. One enterprising Ninja even hid in a small sewer waiting for his victim. When his victim sat on the toilet above, the Ninja killed him with a spear from below!

Wartime spies

When countries are at war, the work of spies is more important than ever. Spies try to find out all about the enemy army – how many soldiers they have, what sort of weapons they possess, and what plans they are devising.

Spies in wartime must make sure nobody suspects them. Unlike a regular soldier, spies have to live, dress, and talk like the enemy they are fighting. But if spies are caught they risk being executed, whereas soldiers are just taken prisoner.

Still, John André thought it was a risk worth taking. In 1780 André was a British spy in the Revolutionary War. He had been told that U.S. General Benedict Arnold would surrender his fort in exchange for a lot of money.

The two men arranged a secret meeting to fix the deal. Under cover of darkness, André left his ship and got into a small boat. Draped in a large black cloak, he was quickly rowed toward enemy territory.

Arnold did not arrive at the agreed time. Minutes ticked by – each one bringing André closer to dawn and the risk of capture.

At last, as dawn was approaching, Arnold appeared and the two men held their meeting. But André had waited so long he had missed the boat that was to take him back to his ship. He would have to walk through enemy lands until he was back in British-held territory.

André hid until darkness fell, then he started his dangerous journey home.

After walking many hours, he saw a British camp in the distance – he was safe! But then disaster struck! Three roving U.S. soldiers caught André and searched him. They found secret papers he had hidden in his boots. The fact that he was not wearing a British uniform proved he was a spy, not a soldier, and he was shot.

Spies worked for both sides in World War II. Britain trained many spies to help the French fight the German army that had invaded France. The spies were often dropped over France at night by parachute, or set down by small boats on remote beaches. All the spies wore disguises and carried false passports and documents to keep their real identities secret from the Germans.

Every mission they undertook was extremely dangerous.

German troops were on the lookout for spies all the time. Spies, if caught, risked torture and even death at the hands of the Germans.

The spies helped the French resistance fighters. Together they blew up trains and bridges and helped to plan attacks on German army bases. Radio operators sent secret messages to Britain with details on German troop movements and weapons. The vital information gathered by these brave spies helped Allied troops liberate France in 1944.

German spies in World War II had a top-secret weapon called Enigma; a unique machine that turned messages into clever codes. The Germans believed that these codes were impossible to crack. Indeed, the coded messages baffled British and U.S. spies for many months. The British knew it was vital to crack these German codes quickly in order to win the war.

A German Enigma machine

Beware of the Bombe

In trying to crack the codes, scientists invented the first ever electronic computer. It was called the Bombe after a type of ice cream they ate!

Britain's top scientists went to work at Bletchley Park, the top-secret spy station, to find the key to Enigma.

They made little progress at first. Then suddenly, their luck turned. An Enigma machine was captured from the Germans. Knowing how it worked would help the scientists in their efforts to crack the code. After months of frustratingly slow work, they finally found the key!

The decoded messages proved invaluable and helped Britain and the U.S. discover vital enemy secrets.

"Peacetime" spies

In the 1950s the world was not at war, but it was not really at peace, either. The United States feared attack by communist countries and built nuclear weapons of terrible power. They aimed the weapons at Russia and other communist countries. The communist countries were just as afraid and built similar weapons. A dangerous rivalry began.

Most countries supported either the U.S. or Russia. People called this time of fear the Cold War. It gave spying new importance. America's spy agency, the Central Intelligence Agency (CIA), tried to discover the strengths of Russian weapons. Russia's spy agency, the KGB, sent spies on similar missions to the U.S. Both tried to capture each other's spies.

A "mushroom" cloud after a nuclear test explosion

When the U.S. built the first nuclear bombs in 1945, the KGB was keen to learn the details. Russian spies were sent to the U.S. to find out all they could.

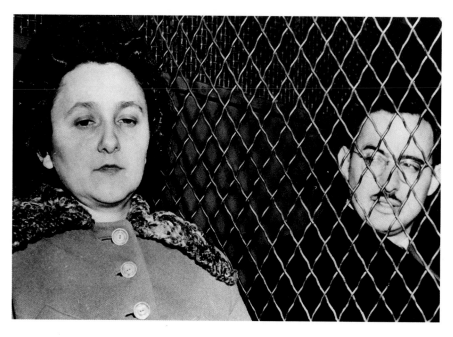

Ethel Rosenberg and her husband, Julius, were Americans who were arrested in 1950 for spying for the KGB. Ethel's brother worked on the bomb and gave her secrets which she passed to the KGB. The Rosenbergs were executed for spying.

But the damage was done. The Russians had all the information they needed and had already made a nuclear bomb.

One of the worst moments in the Cold War was what became known as the Cuban Missile Crisis. Cuba is an island just 90 miles (150 kilometers) south of Florida. In 1962, CIA spies in Cuba noticed that Russian "advisors" there wore only two kinds of shirts – they were soldiers in disguise. Spy planes then spotted Russian missiles on the island. The world was on the brink of World War III. Luckily the Russians backed down.

Smoking is dangerous
The CIA felt that Cuba's leader Fidel Castro was such a threat that they plotted to murder him with a poisoned cigar.

Philby and his mother

Kim Philby was a very successful spy. He worked for Britain's spy service helping to catch Russian spies. He was so respected that he was offered a job in Washington, D.C., teaching spy-catching skills to the CIA. Then, in 1951, two of Philby's friends were caught spying for Russia. They escaped before agents could arrest them. Had Philby warned them? "Of course not!" he said.

But he was lying. Like his two friends, Philby was really spying for Russia. All three men were double agents, pretending to work for one side while secretly spying for the other side.

Philby carried on his treacherous and dangerous double-dealing until 1963.

Just as he was about to be arrested in Beirut, Lebanon he disappeared. Six months later he reappeared as a KGB colonel in Russia!

Kim Philby in Russia with his new Russian wife.

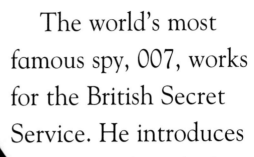

The world's most famous spy, 007, works for the British Secret Service. He introduces himself with the immortal words, "My name is Bond, James Bond." He is the classic gentleman. His manners are perfect. His clothes are never creased. He drives fast, stylish cars. He is licensed to kill. And when this spy kills his enemies, he does it with style.

Bond is also famous for the unique electronic gadgets and clever cars he uses.

Bond and friend escaping

Poison pens
Like James Bond, writer Ian Fleming loved clever and dangerous gadgets. He often carried a pen that sprayed tear gas.

An ejector seat in his car sends unwanted passengers flying through the sunroof. A suitcase-sized helicopter allows him to soar over an enemy's hideaway. Even his watch hides a razor-sharp blade to cut rope.

Although James Bond is not a real spy, his creator was. During World War II, Ian Fleming worked as a spy for the British navy. Many of his own adventures were even more amazing than Bond's, and he based many of his fictional characters on people he had actually met in his years as a spy!

A spy's toolkit

All spies use special tools to do their work. Special cameras give them sharper eyes. Hidden microphones work like super-powerful ears. Ingenious weapons and gadgets help them escape if they are caught.

Tools and gadgets like these make spying much easier. However, they can also land a spy in trouble. In many countries it is forbidden to take pictures of planes, tanks, or soldiers – even in peacetime. Cameras, recorders, and other spying tools could arouse suspicion.

Deadly pencil

This normal-looking pencil actually conceals a sharp and deadly dagger. It could be used by spies to help fight off an enemy agent.

These gadgets are either disguised to look like something an ordinary traveler might carry, or they are made very tiny, so a spy can easily hide them.

This may look like an ordinary briefcase. But inside is an array of secret gadgets, recorders, cameras, and weapons to help make a spy's job easier.

Spies often need evidence to prove that someone is a traitor, or that a country has a new weapon. Pictures are great evidence and spies now have very special cameras. Magnifying lenses allow spies to photograph secret meetings from a long way away. Night-vision lenses turn darkness into daylight.

Soldiers wearing night-vision lenses

The view through a pair of night-vision lenses

When an ordinary camera would make a guard suspicious, spies use tiny cameras no bigger than a matchbox.

Spy cameras first appeared more than 100 years ago. Known as "detective cameras," they were hidden in books, hats, watches – even in loaves of bread!

Super snapper
During World War II this miniature camera, called a Minox, became essential equipment for all spies on active duty.

Spies may have the most up-to-date camera and possess vital details of an enemy's secrets, but pictures and notes are useless until they can be passed on to their bosses.

Today's spies can send pictures or messages by phone, fax, or computer, but it wasn't always as easy. In World War I spies used birds as a secret airmail service. Pigeons flew home with letters tied to their legs or feathers!

With the invention of radio, spies no longer needed pigeons. Instead, they tapped out messages on a clicking key.

Invisible ink
Spies can write in lemon juice to make a secret message. The words disappear when the juice dries – and will reappear when warmed up.

Each group of clicks signified a letter which was sent instantly, not as speech, but as short and long bursts of radio waves. These radios made communication much easier. They also made it more dangerous. Enemy agents could trace the signals straight back to the radio set – placing the operator in danger from capture.

This radio was used by British spies in World War II.

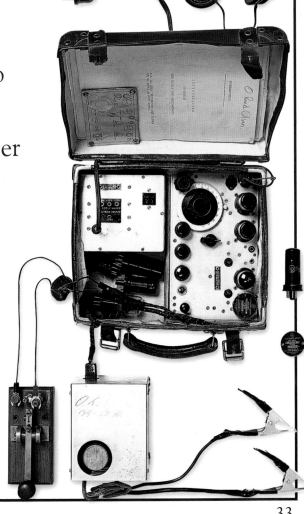

When you make a private phone call, how many people hear it? Just you and the person you are calling? Or is someone else listening too?

Tapping a phone means secretly connecting an extra phone or tape recorder to a phone line. Every time the phone is used, the conversation is automatically transmitted to a special radio receiver.

Telephone taps are not the only way of listening to a private conversation. Bugs – tiny radio sets and microphones – also pick up and transmit speech. They can be hidden anywhere around the house where two people may talk.

Pens that listen

This pen looks like any other, but it contains a tiny secret bug that can be used to listen to and tape a private conversation.

If a house is "bugged," a spy with a radio can hear every word that is said from the safety of a car!

Telephone bug in and out of a phone

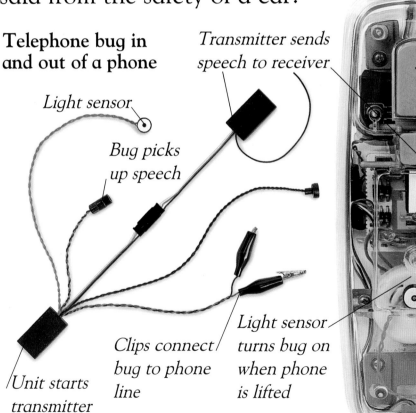

Transmitter sends speech to receiver

Light sensor

Bug picks up speech

Light sensor turns bug on when phone is lifted

Clips connect bug to phone line

Unit starts transmitter working

Bugs work on the same principle as a radio, so it is easy to tell if your home contains one of the simpler types of bugs. Just play some loud music in the suspect room and then tune a radio outside the house. When the radio is tuned to the channel the bug is using, it will play the same music you are playing in the room!

Smart bugs are much harder to find. They switch quickly between lots of channels instead of using just one. They can spread the sounds the microphone picks up across several different channels.

Scramblers

A phone scrambler keeps calls secret. Someone with the same scrambler hears speech, but spies listening in hear only a crackle.

To detect and remove these bugs you need special scanning tools.

Spies can attach a bug to any part of a phone line

Finding telephone taps is tougher still. Sometimes you can see where a spy has cut open phone wires indoors or nearby. But a spy can fit a tap to the line anywhere between the telephone and the telephone exchange, and finding it may be virtually impossible.

Modern spying

Today spies continue to carry out their traditional jobs. But they are also starting to fill a new role – they are fighting crime. Spies have unique skills. They are used to gathering top-secret information. They are used to dealing with dangerous situations. They can defend themselves when they are in danger. They know how to disguise themselves so that they can move around undetected.

Spies are very good at disguise and mingling in a crowd.

Spies are helping the police to catch dangerous criminals.

These special skills can be very valuable to a country's police force. So spies are now working closely with the police in the fight against terrorists, drug smugglers and other dangerous criminals. Whoever they work for, spies have a new and powerful weapon – one that helps them secretly watch people and places from the safety of space!

Satellites are a spy's best friend. They circle high above the Earth, taking continuous pictures of everything happening below. The pictures are then transmitted to computers on the ground.

Spy spotting

Spy satellites may be secret, but they are not invisible! If you look carefully just after dusk, you can sometimes see a satellite slowly moving.

Spies can use the satellite pictures to discover important information. For instance, satellite pictures allowed U.S. spies to locate enemy tanks and soldiers in the 1991 Gulf War.

Some satellites can even take pictures clear enough to count individual soldiers.

At one time, satellite pictures were taken on negative film. When the roll was finished, it fell back to Earth for processing: a U.S. plane flying below caught the film in mid-air! Today's modern satellites use radio signals to beam down their pictures.

This satellite image shows buildings in pink. With enlargement, you can see objects as small as a human.

Spying skills are particularly useful in the fight against drug dealers. A "spy in the sky" can locate drug fields, landing strips, and drug laboratories. This information helps spies to find those who harvest, clean, and transport the drugs. Once enough evidence has been gathered, police can arrest those involved.

Spies also help police track and catch organized-crime gangs. They often go under cover and become members of a group, reporting back to the police on the organization's plans. Information such as how the gang obtains their weapons can help the police defeat the illegal arms trade.

Spies in the CIA work closely with their police counterparts to help combat terrorism in the U.S. and other countries. They helped capture the terrorists who bombed New York's World Trade Center in 1993.

Terror tactics

Around the world, police and spies work together to try and stop terrorists from planting deadly bombs like this one.

Although spies may be helping police beat drug dealers and terrorists, they also have to keep their own houses in order – as one recent case proves.

Aldrich Ames worked for the CIA, where he was in charge of catching Russian spies. In 1985 he was asked to uncover a double agent who had sold the KGB the name of every U.S. spy in Russia. Doubts about Ames began to grow as time went by. Why couldn't he catch the double agent?

Aldrich Ames when he was first arrested

Aldrich Ames on his way to serving a life sentence

CIA chiefs grew suspicious of his lack of success and ordered him to be followed. They filmed him taking top-secret papers and hiding them in hollow trees where Russian spies exchanged the papers for piles of money. Aldrich Ames was the double agent! His double-dealing had made him rich. The U.S. spies he named for money were less lucky. They were executed.

Many of today's spies don't even have to leave home. Instead of traveling overseas, they can turn on a computer and the Internet links them to millions of other computers all around the world.

China has already trained its top spies to wage war using computer viruses.

Every two minutes someone uses the Internet to try to connect to the Pentagon – the U.S. war office. Most of these "attacks" are totally harmless, but not all of them.

Schoolboy spy

A "spy" who broke into U.S. Air Force computers turned out to be Richard Pryce, a brilliant 16-year-old from Britain.

During the war in former Yugoslavia, Serbian experts used the Internet to attack NATO's computers. (NATO is an alliance between a group of countries.) The damage was repaired but, in the future, virus warfare could do as much harm as bombs.

Glossary

Blackmail
Using an embarrassing secret to force someone to do something they don't want to do.

Bugs
Tiny listening devices that allow spies in another place to hear conversations in the room where the bug is hidden.

CIA
Central Intelligence Agency, the spy agency of the U.S.

Code
A secret way of writing a message to hide its real meaning.

Computer virus
A harmful program that spreads from computer to computer.

Disguise
Any way of changing your identity to stop other people from recognizing you.

Double agents
People who pretend to spy for one country while really spying for another country.

Internet
World-wide network of computers used for trade, to provide information, and to send messages.

KGB
The spy agency of the Soviet Union (now Russia).

NATO
North Atlantic Treaty Organization.

Night-vision lenses
Lenses that enable the wearer to see in the dark.

Ninjas
Secret killer spies who stalked Japan eight centuries ago.

Nuclear weapons
Bombs that use radioactive materials to create explosions of enormous power.

Radio waves
Invisible rays that carry sound to distant places.

Resistance fighters
People who secretly fight against the soldiers who have invaded their country.

Revolutionary War
The war (1776-83) that Americans fought to finally end British rule in their country.

Satellites
Spacecraft that constantly circle above the earth, often taking photographs of the land below.

Surrender
To voluntarily stop fighting and give up to your enemies.

Taps
Electronic devices fitted into a phone or a phone line that allow spies to listen to private telephone calls.

Terrorists
People who seek to gain power by frightening others with acts or threats of violence and crime.

Torture
Purposefully causing someone pain to try and make them reveal a secret.

Index